Taking Hearing Impairment to School

by Elaine Ernst Schneider

JayJo Books
Publishing Special Books for Special Kids®

Taking Hearing Impairment to School
© 2004 JayJo Books
Edited by Karen Schader

Published by
JayJo Books
A Brand of the Guidance Group
Publishing Special Books for Special Kids®

JayJo Books is a publisher of books to help teachers, parents, and children cope with chronic illnesses, special needs, and health education in classroom, family, and social settings.

Library of Congress Control Number: 2003114682
ISBN 10: 1-891383-23-X
ISBN 13: 978-1-891383-23-6
First Edition
Fifteenth book in our *Special Kids in School*® series

For all information, including
Premium and Special Sales, contact:
JayJo Books
The Guidance Group
www.guidance-group.com

The opinions in this book are solely those of the author. Medical care is highly individualized and should never be altered without professional medical consultation.

Dedication

This book is dedicated to all my students, past and present,
hearing and hearing impaired, children of my heart;

And to Katie and Nickie, children of my flesh,
and the loves of my life.

Mother, Teacher, Writer
Elaine Ernst Schneider

Hi! My name is Jacob. I live in a big white house with my mom, my dad, and my goldfish, Sam. I also have a dog named Ruff, two cats, a turtle, and a rabbit. I love animals, and I have to get up very early to feed all of mine! Outside, the birds begin to sing at dawn, but I don't hear them. My mom pats me gently on the arm to wake me. I can't hear the birds because I am hearing impaired.

My hearing impairment makes me hear sounds differently than other kids. Sometimes the noises I hear are fuzzy. There are some sounds—like the birds chirping—that I can't hear at all. Still, I've learned not to miss out on anything. I ride my bike, do tricks on my skateboard, and shoot hoops with my friends almost every day!

I pay attention to everything around me. There are always clues that tell me what is going on.

I ride a big yellow bus to school. My school has "special services," like speech therapy. Some kids with hearing impairments come from far away just to go to this school. My friend Joey rides on the bus for an hour!

Speaking clearly is hard for me. Most of the time, I only hear parts of words. So, when I repeat what I've heard, the words are missing the sounds I didn't hear. In speech therapy, the speech-language pathologist shows me how the sounds LOOK. She uses charts and pictures, and even her own mouth! Then I try to make my lips and tongue form the words the correct way.

I really like my school. I'm learning so much!

Mrs. Burns is my classroom teacher. She keeps extra batteries for my hearing aids in her desk. Some kids only wear one hearing aid, but I wear two—one in each ear. They are like tiny microphones that make the sounds I hear louder. I still may not hear everything when I wear my hearing aids, but I do hear much more.

Mrs. Burns knows "sign language," which uses hand motions that stand for words. She uses her hands AND her voice to talk to me. I can understand almost anything when Mrs. Burns explains it. I get clues from her lips, her hands, and her face. I can even tell when she is teasing because I see it in her eyes!

I'm very good at "reading" faces.

There are other hearing-impaired boys and girls in my classroom. Some have only a mild hearing loss. They hear many sounds—just not everything. The kids with a mild loss speak more clearly than I do. My speech therapist says it is because they hear more speech. They learn from listening to other people's words.

My hearing loss is called "profound"; that means it is more than mild. The nerves that carry sounds from my ears to my brain don't work quite right. Without my hearing aids, I can only hear a few sounds. One time, Joey accidentally slammed the door right behind me. I didn't even hear it! I felt a swish of air, though, and I knew what had happened. I quickly turned around and that's when I saw the surprised look on Joey's face. We laughed so hard!

I don't have to hear everything to figure out how things happen. I can understand by seeing and feeling.

I go to math class with kids that hear normally. An interpreter (in-tur-pre-tur) stands near me and signs what everyone in the class says. Mr. Graves, my math teacher, writes almost everything he teaches on the board. It's great because I can see all the steps for each problem.

In math class, seeing is more important than hearing. My eyes give my brain information. And my brain just goes WILD with numbers! Math is my favorite class of the day.

I'd tell you that I'm really good at math—but then I might be bragging!

Some of the hearing kids in my math class are learning sign language. Mr. Graves is too! Sign language helps us talk with each other. I like finding out what my friends did over the weekend or talking about the latest movies.

Not all of my friends and family sign. But I can understand most of what they are saying by reading their lips. They just have to remember to face me and to make sure I can see their mouths.

I can't read your lips if all I can see is the back of your head!

A lot of kids with hearing loss go to special language arts classes. Some hearing-impaired boys and girls go to tutoring. Other kids—like me—do both. I have problems with writing sentences. Because I don't hear all the phrases people say, I'm never very sure how sentences should go together. Mrs. Benton is my language teacher. She uses different colored blocks to make sentence patterns. Each color stands for a part of a sentence. I like the red "verb" blocks the best.

Miss Tucker is my tutor. She is really good at computer games! Miss Tucker has a game where I have to arrange the words in a sentence correctly before a light blinks. It's so exciting when I beat the game and win!

I like my language arts teacher and my tutor. They are helping me learn to communicate in writing.

Once a year, I visit an audiologist (aw-dee-ol-oh-gist) for hearing tests. An audiologist tests hearing and helps people with hearing loss to hear better. The tests help the audiologist make a chart called an audiogram. It is a good way to show my doctor, my teachers, my parents, and me what I can hear. My audiologist also makes sure that my hearing aids are working well, and tells me about new or different hearing aids that may help me hear even better.

Scientists are always finding ways to make things better, including hearing aids. Maybe one day they will invent an aid that will help me hear EVERYTHING!

Once, I went to see an educational psychologist (si-col-oh-gist). An educational psychologist helps kids find out how much they know. She gave me a test that had pictures instead of words. It was the perfect test for me, because I know so much stuff that I don't have words for! The psychologist told my parents and my teachers that I am very smart.

My dad said he'd known that all along!

I can't change that I'm hearing impaired—but I can learn different ways to do things! My dad is helping me. He installed a special doorbell at our house. When someone rings it, a light blinks in the hall. Then I know we have visitors. Once a month, my scout troop meets at our house. The light blinks on and off as the boys and their dads come to the door.

My family also has a telephone with a keyboard. I can "talk" on the phone by typing what I want to say! An operator sends my message to the person I called and then types back an answer.

I can "talk" to my grandma on our special phone. She always messages back, "I love you."

Scientists and doctors are working hard to discover ways to help hearing-impaired kids—and adults—live with hearing loss. Maybe there will be a way that I can hear better when I am grown up. But for now, there are animals to feed and baseball games to play!

Right now, Ruff and I are going outside to play with Joey.

LET'S TAKE THE HEARING IMPAIRMENT KIDS' QUIZ!

1. **What is hearing impairment?**
   Hearing impairment is a condition that makes me hear things differently than I should. Noises may be distorted or fuzzy, and I may not be able to hear some sounds at all.

2. **Is hearing impairment contagious?**
   No, you cannot catch hearing impairment from me or anyone else.

3. **How can you talk with a hearing-impaired friend?**
   You can learn sign language if your friend signs. Or you can talk and let your friend read your lips. Remember to look each other in the face and talk normally—you don't need to yell.

4. **What does an audiologist do?**
   An audiologist tests hearing. Charts are made from the test results that show what the person can hear. An audiologist may suggest hearing aids.

5. **What is speech therapy?**
   I go to speech therapy to work on saying sounds and words. The speech-language pathologist shows me how the sounds look so that I can try to form them correctly when I talk.

6. **Can hearing-impaired kids attend hearing classes?**

   Yes. In some courses, like math, kids use their eyes more than their ears. Hearing-impaired students do well in these classes with an interpreter.

7. **What does an interpreter do?**

   An interpreter uses his or her hands to sign what someone says.

8. **Why do hearing-impaired kids go to special language arts classes?**

   Kids with hearing loss don't hear all the words that people say, so we are not sure how sentences should go together. Lessons and games that teach sentence structure help us to write better.

9. **Can hearing-impaired kids play sports?**

   Sure, they can! I love baseball. I have friends who play football, volleyball, and basketball.

10. **Will scientists and doctors find new ways to help kids with hearing loss hear better someday?**

    No one knows, but they will keep working to discover new ways to deal with hearing impairment.

Ten Tips for Teachers

✓ **1. SEAT STUDENTS WHO ARE HEARING IMPAIRED NEAR THE FRONT OF THE CLASSROOM.**

Because children who are hearing impaired depend on clues from their visual environment, arrange the desks so that these children are near where you will be teaching.

✓ **2. AVOID TURNING YOUR BACK WHILE SPEAKING, EVEN TO WRITE ON A CHALK BOARD.**

An overhead projector will allow you the freedom of writing notes or illustrating problems while still facing the class.

✓ **3. UNDERSTAND THAT STUDENTS WHO ARE HEARING IMPAIRED WILL STRUGGLE WITH SENTENCE SYNTAX.**

Look for concepts when reading the student's written work in all fields of studies, except language arts. Correct syntax in science, social studies, or math word problems, but reward the student for factual knowledge in these subject areas, praising him or her for knowing the information. Language arts class should provide a concentrated focus on sentence patterns and other writing skills.

✓ **4. WORK CLOSELY WITH THE LANGUAGE ARTS TEACHER, SPEECH-LANGUAGE PATHOLOGIST, AND TUTOR.**

Coordinated efforts benefit students who are hearing impaired. For example, the speech-language pathologist or language tutor can reinforce vocabulary word lists from the subject area teacher. Additionally, subject area teachers may find the language arts teacher a valuable resource for helping the student with language-related assignments, like reports.

✓ **5. INCLUDE STUDENTS WHO ARE HEARING IMPAIRED IN GROUP PROJECTS.**

Children will invariably find ways to communicate. Creating situations that combine hearing and non-hearing students fosters the desire to communicate. Group projects open up the hearing world to the child who is hearing impaired, introducing him or her to the norms of a hearing society. Hearing students learn to look beyond impairment and to appreciate the person each child is "on the inside."

6. MODIFY! MODIFY! MODIFY!

Adapt textbooks and other materials to incorporate high-interest facts with low-level vocabulary. Don't be afraid to modify tests so that the results reflect the student's knowledge rather than his disability.

7. WELCOME THE INTERPRETER'S HELP.

While most interpreters are not teachers, they are trained in turning the spoken word into a conceptual sign that the student who is hearing impaired can understand. Don't be afraid to let the interpreter add explanation.

8. CONNECT WITH PARENTS.

Parents of children who are hearing impaired may or may not be hearing impaired themselves. When you arrange the initial meeting with your student's parents, determine whether an interpreter will be needed. If the parents are dependent upon the interpreter to translate your words into signs, pause momentarily after groups of thoughts to allow the interpreter to catch up. Use this meeting with the parents to discuss goals for the student, parental expectations, and ways in which parents can reinforce learning at home. Decide on a time and method for follow-up contact.

9. GET TO KNOW YOUR STUDENT.

Try to understand the student who is hearing impaired as a "whole child." Appreciate the sense of humor, artistic talent, or athletic ability that makes the student who he or she is, apart from hearing loss. Participate in the student's life in areas other than those you teach. Compliment achievements in gym class, and ask about the child's weekend. You will find that most students who are hearing impaired are "regular" kids with active lives.

10. CELEBRATE SUCCESSES!

Rejoice in each triumph. Encouragement translates into motivation.

ADDITIONAL RESOURCES

National Institute on Deafness and Other Communication Disorders
National Institutes of Health
31 Center Drive, MSC 2320
Bethesda, MD 20892-2320
1-800-241-1044
www.nidcd.nih.gov/about/learn/index.asp

American Speech-Language-Hearing Association
10801 Rockville Pike
Rockville, MD 20852
1-800-638-8255
www.asha.org/about/contacts.cfm

The Council for Exceptional Children
1110 North Glebe Road, Suite 300
Arlington, VA 22201-5704
1-888-CEC-SPED
www.cec.sped.org/

Laurent Clerc National Deaf Education Center
Gallaudet University
800 Florida Ave. NE
Washington, DC 20002
1-202-651-5051
http://clerccenter.gallaudet.edu/InfoToGo/

National Association of the Deaf
814 Thayer Avenue
Silver Spring, MD 20910-4500
1-301-587-1788 Voice
www.nad.org/

American Society for Deaf Children
P.O. Box 3355
Gettysburg, PA 17325
1-800-942-ASDC
www.deafchildren.org/hom/home/hrml

To order additional copies of this book or inquire about our quantity discounts for schools, hospitals, and affiliated organizations, contact us at 1-800-999-6884.

From our *Special Kids in School*® series
Taking A.D.D. to School
Taking Arthritis to School
Taking Asthma to School
Taking Autism to School
Taking Cancer to School
Taking Cerebral Palsy to School
Taking Cystic Fibrosis to School
Taking Depression to School
Taking Diabetes to School
Taking Down Syndrome to School
Taking Dyslexia to School
Taking Food Allergies to School
Taking Hearing Impairment to School
Taking Seizure Disorders to School
Taking Speech Disorders to School
Taking Tourette Syndrome to School
Taking Visual Impairment to School
Taking Weight Problems to School

Other books available now!
SPORTSercise!
A School Story about
Exercise-Induced Asthma
ZooAllergy
A Fun Story about Allergy
and Asthma Triggers
Rufus Comes Home
Rufus the Bear with Diabetes™
A Story about Diagnosis and Acceptance
The ABC's of Asthma
An Asthma Alphabet Book
for Kids of All Ages
Trick-or-Treat for Diabetes
A Halloween Story for Kids
Living with Diabetes

From our *Healthy Habits for Kids*® series
There's a Louse in My House
A Fun Story about Kids and Head Lice

From our *Special Family and Friends*™ series
Allie Learns About Alzheimer's Disease
A Family Story about Love, Patience,
and Acceptance
Patrick Learns About Parkinson's Disease
A Story of a Special Bond Between Friends
Dylan Learns About Diabetes
A Story of a Support and Understanding

And from our *Substance Free Kids*® series
Smoking STINKS!!™
A Heartwarming Story about the
Importance of Avoiding Tobacco